D1252706

Doves are common throughout the world

Doves

Jill Kalz

A^{+}

Smart Apple Media

COPYRIGHT

Published by Smart Apple Media

1980 Lookout Drive, North Mankato, MN 56003

Designed by Rita Marshall

Copyright © 2003 Smart Apple Media. International copyright reserved in all countries. No part of this book may be reproduced in any form without written permission from the publisher.

Printed in the United States of America

Photographs by Brian Gosewisch, JLM Visuals (Richard P. Jacobs), KAC Productions (Kathy Adams Clark, Bill Draker, Glenn Hayes), Sally Myers, Tom Myers, Root Resources (Glenn Jahnke)

Library of Congress Cataloging-in-Publication Data

Kalz, Jill. Doves / by Jill Kalz. p. cm. – (Birds) 440

Includes bibliographical references and index.

Summary: Describes the physical characteristics, behavior, and habitat of doves.

ISBN 1-58340-128-8   1. Doves—J.

1. Columbidae—Juvenile literature. [1. Pigeons.] I. Title.

QL696.C63 K35 2002   598.6'5—dc21   2001049675

First Edition 9 8 7 6 5 4 3 2 1

Doves

CONTENTS

Hope and Peace

When most people hear the word "dove," they think

of small white birds. But doves come in many sizes and colors.

Plump gray pigeons are actually doves too. There are

close to 300 different kinds, or species, of doves in the world.

(Larger species are usually called pigeons, and smaller species

are called doves.) About 12 species live in the United States

and Canada. Doves are often used as symbols of hope

and peace. They appear in many religious stories, including the

Biblical story of Noah. After the Great Flood, Noah sent a dove

from his ark in search of dry land. The dove returned with an

olive branch. This told Noah that the flood had ended and that

there was hope for the future of the world.

White is one of many dove colors

Dove Details

Doves make their homes in many different places.

Forests, deserts, prairies, backyards, and cities are some of their

favorite habitats. They can live just about *An adult female dove is called a hen; an adult male is called a cock.*

anywhere, except the North and South Poles.

One of the smallest doves in the world

measures just seven and a half inches (19 cm)

long. The largest is the blue-crowned pigeon of New Guinea.

At 33 inches (84 cm) long, it is about the size of a small turkey.

Most doves have small heads, plump bodies covered with

soft feathers, and thick, fleshy legs. Long toes help doves bal-

ance while walking or perching. Doves often bob their heads

and coo while they walk. Cooing is the doves' way of "talking" to

A blue-crowned pigeon

A family of mourning doves

other doves. Gray and brown are the dove's most common **plumage** colors. But some doves are quite colorful, especially around their necks. The common pigeon has gray plumage, a white rump, and brilliant green and purple neck feathers. A dove's beak, or bill, is straight, with a slightly down-turned tip. Doves use their beaks to eat

Doves eat bits of sand to help them digest seeds in a part of their stomach called the gizzard.

seeds, fruits and berries, leaves, and insects. City-dwelling doves may also eat popcorn or bread crumbs lying on the sidewalk.

Dove plumage in shades of gray and brown

Eggs to Chicks

In the fall, some doves **migrate** to warmer climates. They may fly only a short distance or travel all the way from southern Canada to Mexico. When they return in the spring, doves look for mates. Males try to attract females by spreading their tails like fans, strutting, and cooing.

Most doves are very strong flyers; homing pigeons can zoom along at 82 miles (132 km) per hour!

 Once doves have mated, they build a nest. Dove nests are made of twigs and can be found on the ground, inside trees and cliff walls, or atop barn rafters, bridges, or buildings.

The female lays one or two white eggs. The male and female

doves take turns warming them. After about two weeks, the

eggs hatch. The baby doves, or chicks, punch their way out of

Nests are well-hidden to protect chicks

their shells using a special "egg tooth" that falls out shortly after they hatch. Newly hatched dove chicks are completely helpless. They do not have any feathers, their eyes are closed, and they cannot feed themselves. But with good care from their parents, baby doves develop a full set of feathers in just two weeks. One week after that, they are on their own.

Dove chicks are fed "pigeon's milk," a thick liquid made inside a special pouch in their parents' throats.

A three-week-old baby dove

Past and Future

The world can be a dangerous place for a small bird.

Dove eggs and chicks may be snatched from nests by raccoons

or snakes. Adult doves may fly into wires

or they may be attacked by larger birds

such as hawks. But the biggest threat to

doves is people. In the early 1800s,

The last passenger pigeon on Earth died in the Cincinnati Zoo on September 1, 1914; her name was "Martha."

three to five billion passenger pigeons lived in North America.

Today, they are **extinct**. These birds once made their nests in

the forests of eastern North America. As settlers moved in, they

chopped down trees and destroyed the pigeon's habitat.

Hunters also shot huge numbers of the birds for food and

sport. Sadly, by 1914, all of the passenger pigeons were gone.

A raccoon, one of the dove's enemies

Although some doves, such as the common pigeon, are widespread and thriving today, many other species of doves are in danger of becoming extinct. Thankfully, special groups of people, called **conservationists**, are working hard to protect doves and dove habitats. With their help, there is hope that we may be able to keep more doves from disappearing forever.

Today, people around the world raise pigeons to race them, to show them in competitions, and to eat them.

The bleeding heart pigeon's unusual plumage

Dove Breakfast Cake

Most doves in North America are seed eaters. Ask an adult to help you make this seed-filled treat and see how many doves—and other birds—fly in for breakfast.

What You Need

A freshly mixed bowl of cornbread batter
One egg
One cup (275 ml) birdseed (preferably with black oil sunflower or thistle seeds)
An oven
A baking pan (check the cornbread mix package for size)
A pie tin

What You Do

1. Add the egg to the batter. Crumble the eggshell and add it to the batter too.
2. Mix in the birdseed. If the batter gets too dry, add a little water.
3. Pour the batter into the pan and bake as directed on the cornbread mix package.
4. Allow the cake to cool, then crumble a slice onto the pie tin. (You can freeze the rest.) Set the tin outside and watch the birds come to feed!

Doves love to eat seeds and berries

INFORMATION

Index

Words to Know

conservationists (kon-sir-VAY-shun-ists)—people dedicated to preserving natural resources such as animal habitats

extinct (ek-STINKT)—no longer living anywhere on Earth

habitats (HAB-i-tats)—the areas where certain animals naturally live

migrate (MY-grate)—to move from one area to another according to the changing seasons

plumage (PLOO-mij)—a bird's feathers

Read More

McDonald, MaryAnn. *Doves*. Chanhassen, Minn.: The Child's World, 1999.

Nofsinger, Ray, and Jim Hargrove. *Pigeons and Doves*. N.p.: Children's Press, 1992.

Patent, Dorothy Hinshaw. *Pigeons*. New York: Houghton Mifflin, 1994.

Internet Sites

About.com, Inc.: Birding/Wild Birds
http://birding.about.com/hobbies/
birding

Kid Info: Birds
http://www.kidinfo.com/science/
birds.html

eNature.com
http://www.eNature.com/guides/
select_birds.asp